Usborne
Christmas
Baking
for
Children

Fiona Patchett

Illustrated by Nancy Leschnikoff

Designed by Nelupa Hussain

Recipe consultants: Catherine Atkinson and Dagmar Vesely
American editor: Carrie Armstrong
US cooking consultant: Barbara Tricinella

Contents

Allergy-free recipes

Ⓦ wheat-free   Ⓖ gluten-free

Ⓓ dairy-free   Ⓔ egg-free

Ⓝ contains nuts

Recipes marked with a ✱ have special instructions you will need to follow to make them allergy-free.

Getting started

Before you start cooking, read through the following few pages for some basic baking skills. Then read the recipe, make sure you have all the ingredients and equipment you need and start baking.

Measuring

It's important that you measure things out exactly and don't leave anything out, otherwise your cakes and cookies might not turn out quite right.

Measure dry ingredients in measuring cups and spoons, and measure liquids in a measuring cup. For small amounts, use measuring spoons.

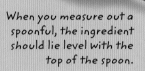

When you measure out a spoonful, the ingredient should lie level with the top of the spoon.

Always use the size and shape of pan suggested in the recipe.

Your oven

Bake things on the middle shelf of your oven. Don't open the oven door while you're cooking, unless the recipe tells you to, or if you think something might be burning. Remember to put on oven mitts before you pick up anything hot.

Keeping clean

You'll find it much easier if you try to clean up as you go along. Put things away after you've used them. If you spill anything, wipe it up right away. And always wash your hands before you start.

If the recipe lists softened butter, take it out of the refrigerator 30 minutes before you use it.

Baking skills

There are many simple skills that cooks use when they are baking. Here are some that will help you make the recipes in this book.

Breaking an egg

Crack the shell sharply on the edge of a bowl. Push your thumbs into the crack and pull the shell apart, so the egg falls into the bowl.

Beating eggs

Use a fork.

Stir the eggs quickly to mix the whites and yolks together.

Separating eggs

Break an egg onto a plate. Cover the yolk with a cup and hold it, while you tip the plate so the white slides off.

Whisking egg whites

① Pour the egg whites into a clean, dry bowl, making sure no yolk gets in. Hold the bowl tightly.

② You can try using a whisk, or use an electric mixer to whisk the eggs until stiff points or 'peaks' form on top, like this.

Grating

Be careful not to scrape your fingers.

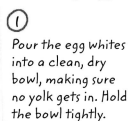

Hold the food you are grating firmly. Scrape it across the holes again and again. Use the small holes for orange or lemon zest.

Squeezing

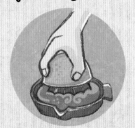

Cut the fruit in half. Press one half at a time onto a citrus squeezer. Twist as you press.

Sifting

Put the powdered sugar, flour or cocoa in a sieve over a bowl. Then shake the sieve.

Beating a mixture

Stir the mixture quickly with a wooden spoon. Continue until the mixture is smooth.

Folding in

Slice through the ingredients with a metal spoon and gently turn them over and over until they are evenly mixed.

Rubbing in

Use your fingers to rub the butter into the flour. Lift the mixture and let it fall back into the bowl as you rub. Continue until the mixture looks like fine breadcrumbs.

Rolling out

Dust the surface and rolling pin with flour.

① Put the dough onto a clean, dry surface. Press the rolling pin onto it and roll away from you.

②  Turn the dough around a little and roll again. Continue until the dough is the thickness you need.

Greasing and lining

To grease a pan, dip a paper towel into some softened butter or cooking oil. Rub it over the inside of the pan.

To line a pan, put it on some baking parchment. Draw around it with a pencil. Cut just inside the line. Lay the parchment in the pan.

Turning out cakes

① When the pan is cool, run a knife around the sides of the pan. Choose a plate slightly larger than the pan and hold it over the pan.

②  Turn the pan and plate over together, so the cake turns out onto the plate. Then, lift the pan off the cake.

Christmas cookies

These vanilla cookies are very simple to make. Cut them into Christmas shapes and decorate them with icing and sugar sprinkles.

Ingredients:

1/2 cup (1 stick) butter, softened

1/2 cup powdered sugar

1 medium egg

1 teaspoon vanilla

1 3/4 cups all-purpose flour

1/4 teaspoon salt

For the icing:

See the recipe for buttercream on page 43.

You will also need:

some shaped cookie cutters

sugar sprinkles to decorate

❄ Makes around 35 cookies.

1. Grease two baking trays. Then, put the butter in a large bowl. Beat it until it is smooth. Use a sieve to sift in the powdered sugar. Beat again.

2. Break the egg into a small bowl. Add the vanilla and beat well with a fork.

3. Add the eggy mixture to the large bowl, a little at a time. Beat well between each addition.

4. Add the flour and salt. Stir the mixture until it starts to form a dough. Then, use your hands to mix the dough and squeeze it into a ball.

5. Wrap the dough in plastic foodwrap and put it in the refrigerator for 30 minutes. Preheat the oven to 350°F.

6. Unwrap the dough and put it onto a clean surface. Roll it out until it is just thinner than your little finger. Use the cutters to cut out lots of shapes.

Dust the surface and a rolling pin with flour.

7

Put the cookies onto the trays. Squeeze the scraps together and roll them out again. Cut out more shapes and put them on the trays.

8

Bake for 8-10 minutes until golden. Leave on the trays for 5 minutes, then put on a wire rack to cool.

9

For the icing, sift the powdered sugar into a bowl. Stir in the butter, milk and vanilla. Spread onto each cookie with a blunt knife. Scatter sugar sprinkles on top.

These will keep for up to 5 days in an airtight container.

You could add different flavors to your cookies. Here are some suggestions. Leave out the vanilla and, at step 4, add:

❉ 1 teaspoon of ground cinnamon

❉ 2 teaspoons of ground ginger or orange zest

Lemon cinnamon stars

These delicious and chewy cookies are flavored with cinnamon and lemon.
They are popular in Switzerland, Austria and Germany, where they
are known as 'Zimtsterne', meaning cinnamon stars.

Ingredients:

2 lemons

2¹/₂ cups powdered sugar

3 cups (14 oz.) ground almonds

2 teaspoons ground cinnamon

2 medium eggs

For the lemon glaze:

¹/₄ cup powdered sugar

1¹/₂ tablespoons lemon juice

You will also need:

a small star-shaped cutter

❄ Makes around 40 stars.

1
Preheat the oven to 400°F. Line a baking tray with baking parchment or use non-stick cooking spray. Grate the zest from the lemons.

2
Sift the powdered sugar into a large bowl. Mix it with the lemon zest, ground almonds and cinnamon.

3
Separate the eggs. Put the whites into a large, clean bowl. Use an electric mixer to whisk them until they are really thick. They should make stiff peaks, like this.

You don't need the yolks.

4
Gently fold the almond mixture into the egg whites to make a stiff dough. If it's too sticky, add more ground almonds.

Dust the surface and rolling pin with powdered sugar.

5
Put the dough onto a work surface and roll it out until it is as thick as your little finger.

6
Use the cutter to cut out star shapes and put them on the baking tray.

You could decorate these cookies with lemon zest. Use a zester to get long curls of zest.

⑦ Bake for 5-6 minutes. Leave on the tray for a few minutes, then put them on a wire rack to cool.

⑧ For the glaze, cut the lemon in half. Squeeze the juice into a small bowl. Sift over the powdered sugar and mix. Spread onto the stars.

These will keep for up to 5 days in an airtight container.

9

Shortbread

Shortbread was traditionally eaten in Scotland at New Year, and the round shape was supposed to look like the sun. But now, shortbread is popular all year, around the world.

Ingredients:

1 1/2 cups all-purpose flour
1/2 cup (1 stick) butter, chilled
1/4 cup sugar
2/3 cup (4 oz.) white chocolate chips
sugar stars to decorate (optional)

You will also need:

an 8 inch round cake pan

❄ Makes 8 slices.

1 Preheat the oven to 300°F. Grease the pan. Add the flour to a large bowl.

2 Cut the butter into chunks. Rub it into the flour until the mixture looks like fine breadcrumbs. Stir in the sugar.

3 Squeeze the mixture into a ball. The heat from your hands makes the dough stick together.

4 Press the mixture into the pan with your fingers. Use the back of a spoon to smooth the top and make it level.

5 Use a fork to press a pattern around the edge. Then, cut the mixture into 8 equal pieces.

6 Bake for 30 minutes until golden. Leave in the pan for 5 minutes. Then cut across it again and put the pieces on a wire rack to cool.

8

Put the chocolate in a heatproof bowl. Carefully put it into the pan. Stir the chocolate until it melts. Lift the bowl out of the pan.

7

Pour some water into a pan, so it's about 1 inch deep. Heat until it bubbles, then turn off the heat.

9

Dip each piece of shortbread into the chocolate, then put onto a sheet of wax paper on a plate. Put in the refrigerator for 20 minutes to set.

You could decorate your shortbread with store-bought sugar stars.

This will keep for up to 5 days in an airtight container.

Chocolate orange hearts

When you bite into these crispy chocolate hearts, you'll find a rich orange filling inside.

Ingredients:

1 cup self-rising flour

4 tablespoons cocoa powder

1/2 cup (1 stick) butter, chilled

1/3 cup sugar

1 egg

For the orange filling:

1/4 cup sugar

2 oz. ground almonds

2 oranges

You will also need:

a heart-shaped cutter,
   at least 2 inches across

❄ Makes around 15 cookies.

1 Grease a baking tray. Mix the flour and cocoa in a large bowl. Cut the butter into chunks and add it to the mixture.

2 Rub the butter into the flour until it looks like breadcrumbs. Stir in the sugar. Separate the egg and stir in the yolk. Put the egg white in a cup to use later.

3 Squeeze together to make a ball of dough. Wrap it in foodwrap. Put it in the refrigerator for 20 minutes.

4 For the filling, put half the egg white in a bowl with the sugar and ground almonds.

5 Grate the zest from the oranges. Add it to the bowl and mix everything together well.

Dust your hands with powdered sugar.

6 Take a teaspoon of the mixture. Roll it into a ball, then flatten it slightly. Make 15 balls. Preheat the oven to 400°F.

Dust the rolling pin and surface with powdered sugar.

7

Take the dough out of the refrigerator. Roll it out until it is as thick as your little finger. Press hard as you roll.

8

Cut out 30 hearts. Put half on the tray. Put a ball of filling on each one. Brush the edges with egg white. Put a second heart on top and press the edges together.

9

Bake for 8-10 minutes. Leave on the tray for a few minutes, then put on a wire rack to cool.

These chocolate orange hearts look pretty if you sift powdered sugar over them.

These will keep for up to 5 days in an airtight container.

Stained-glass windows

These cookies look lovely with light shining through them. You could decorate them with glaze or writing icing, and hang them on a Christmas tree.

Ingredients:

1/2 cup soft light brown sugar

1/3 cup butter, softened

1 small egg

1 1/4 cups all-purpose flour

1 teaspoon allspice

20 see-through hard candies

You will also need:

a large shaped cookie cutter
   (stars or snowflakes look good)

a drinking straw

a small round cutter, slightly bigger
   than the candy

❄ Makes around 20 cookies.

① Preheat the oven to 350°F. Grease and line a baking tray or use non-stick cooking spray.

② Beat the sugar and butter in a large bowl. Break the egg into a small bowl and beat it. Mix half the egg into the butter and sugar. You don't need the other half.

③ Stir in the flour and allspice. Mix everything together really well.

④ Squeeze the mixture together with your hands to form a ball of dough.

Dust the surface and rolling pin with flour.

⑤ Roll out the dough until it is as thick as your little finger. Use the large cutter to cut out shapes. Lift them onto the tray with a spatula.

⑥ Make a hole in each cookie by pressing the straw through the dough, near the top of each one.

To decorate your cookies, you could cover them with glaze (see page 44) or draw on patterns with writing icing. If you're going to hang them up, leave them to dry first and don't eat them afterward — they might be dirty.

These will keep for up to 4 days in an airtight container.

⑦ Use the small, round cutter to cut a hole in the middle of each cookie.

⑧ Squeeze the scraps together and roll them out again. Cut out more cookies.

⑨ Put a candy into the hole in the middle of each cookie. Bake for 12 minutes. Leave on the tray until they are cold.

Linz cookies

These delicious hazelnut cookies are from the city of Linz in Austria. They have a shaped hole cut in the top so the raspberry jam filling shows through.

Ingredients:

$2/3$ cup (4 oz.) hazelnuts

$1\,3/4$ cups all-purpose flour

$3/4$ cup sugar

$3/4$ cup butter, chilled

1 medium egg

$1/2$ teaspoon vanilla

raspberry jam (or any flavor)

You will also need:

a $2\,1/2$ inch round cutter

small cutters in different shapes

✻ Makes around 14 cookies.

① Put the nuts into a plastic food bag and seal the end. Use a rolling pin to crush them into small pieces.

② Put the nuts, flour and sugar into a large bowl. Cut the butter into chunks and rub it into the flour until it looks like breadcrumbs.

③ Separate the egg. Put the yolk into the bowl and add the vanilla. Mix everything together until it forms a dough.

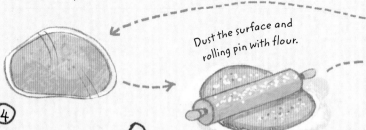

Dust the surface and rolling pin with flour.

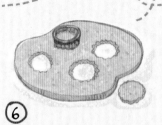

④ Wrap the dough in foodwrap. Put it in the refrigerator to chill for 30 minutes.

⑤ Preheat the oven to 400°F. Line two baking trays or use non-stick cooking spray. Roll out the dough until it is as thick as your little finger.

⑥ Use the round cutter to cut out lots of circles. Squeeze the scraps into a ball. Roll it out and cut more circles.

⑦ Use the small cutter to cut holes in half of the circles. Put all the circles onto the trays and bake for 8 minutes.

⑧ Take the cookies out of the oven. Leave them on the tray for 2 minutes, then put them on a wire rack to cool.

⑨ Spread jam on the whole cookies, as far as the edge. Place a cut-out cookie on each one and press it down gently.

These will keep for up to 5 days in an airtight container.

Mince pies

Mince pies have been a Christmas treat in Britain for centuries. Mincemeat used to contain real meat as well as fruit, but now it's made from fruits and spices. In Britain, some people put out a mince pie on Christmas Eve to thank Santa Claus for their presents.

Ingredients:

For the mincemeat:

1 orange

1 lemon

1/2 cup (3 oz.) seedless grapes

2 1/2 tablespoons (1 oz.) hazelnuts (optional)

1 apple

1 cup (5 oz.) raisins

ground cinnamon, nutmeg and ginger

For the orange crust:

1 medium orange

1 medium egg

1 cup and 2 tablespoons all-purpose flour

1/4 cup powdered sugar

1/2 cup (1 stick) butter

You will also need:

a 12-hole muffin tray

a 2 1/2 inch round cutter

a 2 inch round cutter

❄ Makes 12 mince pies.

These will keep for up to 3 days in an airtight container.

1

Follow the steps on page 43 to make the mincemeat. For the crust, grate the zest from the orange. Then squeeze the juice from half the orange.

Save the egg white to use later.

2

Separate the egg and put the yolk into a small bowl. Mix in the zest and two teaspoons of orange juice.

3

Put the flour and sugar into a large bowl. Cut the butter into chunks and rub it into the flour, until it looks like fine breadcrumbs.

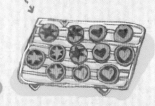

You could sift powdered sugar over your mince pies, if you like.

④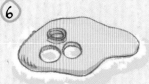

Stir in the orange mixture to make the dough. Wrap in foodwrap and put in the refrigerator for 30 minutes. Preheat the oven to 375° F.

Dust the surface and rolling pin with flour.

⑤ Put the crust onto a clean surface. Roll over it once. Turn it a quarter of the way around and roll over it again. Continue until it's as thick as your little finger.

⑥ Use the large round cutter to cut out 12 circles. Put one in each hole in the tray. Squeeze the scraps together and roll them out. Use the small round cutter to cut 6 lids.

⑦

Use the shaped cutter to cut holes in the 6 lids. Then, spoon a heaped teaspoon of mincemeat into each pastry case.

⑧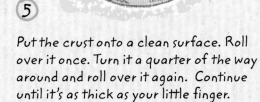

Put lids with cut-out shapes onto half the pies. Put the small shapes on the others. Brush the pastry with the egg white you saved.

⑨ Bake for 20 minutes until golden. Leave in the tray for a few minutes. Then, put them on a wire rack to cool.

White chocolate brownies

Made with white chocolate and tangy cranberries, these brownies are a pale and interesting alternative to traditional brownies. Crispy on top and gooey inside, they are good eaten while they are still slightly warm.

Ingredients:

$1^1/_2$ cups white chocolate chips

6 tablespoons butter

3 medium eggs

$^3/_4$ cup sugar

1 teaspoon vanilla

$1^1/_3$ cups all-purpose flour

pinch of salt

$^1/_2$ cup (3 oz.) dried cranberries

You will also need:

an 8 inch square cake pan

❄ Makes around 25 squares.

These will keep for up to 4 days in an airtight container.

① Preheat the oven to 350°F. Grease and line the pan. Pour 2 inches of water into a pan and heat it gently. When it bubbles, take it off the heat.

② Put half the chocolate chips into a heatproof bowl with the butter, cut into chunks. Carefully, put the bowl into the pan.

③ Stir until the butter and chocolate have melted. Lift the bowl out of the pan.

④ Beat the eggs in a large bowl. Stir in the sugar and vanilla. Add the chocolate mixture a little at a time, beating well between each addition.

⑤ Fold in the flour, salt, cranberries and the rest of the chocolate chips.

⑥ Spoon the mixture into the pan. Bake for 25 minutes for soft, gooey brownies, or 30 minutes to make them firmer.

⑦ Leave in the pan for 20 minutes. Then, cut into little squares. Sift powdered sugar over the top, if you like.

You could add different ingredients to your brownies, instead of cranberries. Here are some suggestions. At step 5, try adding:

✳ chopped crystallized ginger

✳ tiny cubes of marzipan

✳ mini marshmallows

✳ chopped macadamia nuts, hazelnuts, pecans or walnuts

✳ semi-sweet or milk chocolate chips or chunks

21

Christmas cupcakes

These pretty cupcakes are drizzled with the juice of Christmassy oranges, then covered with a thick layer of sweet glaze.

Ingredients:

For the cupcakes:

2 oranges or tangerines

1/2 cup sugar

7 tablespoons butter, softened

2 medium eggs

3/4 cup self-rising flour

For the glaze:

1 1/2 cups powdered sugar

1 1/2 tablespoons warm water

You will also need:

a 12-hole shallow muffin tray

8 paper cupcake cases

❄ Makes 8 cupcakes.

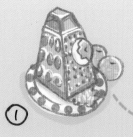

① Preheat the oven to 375°F. Put a paper case in each hole in the tray. Grate the zest from the oranges.

② Beat the sugar, butter and zest in a large bowl. Break the eggs into a cup. Add the eggs and flour to the bowl. Beat until everything is well mixed.

③ Use a spoon to divide the mixture between the cases. Bake for 15 minutes until risen and firm.

④ Squeeze the juice from the oranges. Spoon it over the cupcakes while they are still warm.

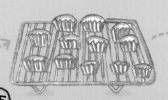

⑤ Put the cupcakes on a wire rack. Leave them until they are cool, then make the glaze.

⑥ Sift the powdered sugar into a bowl and mix it with the warm water. Spread onto each cake with a blunt knife.

These will keep for up to 4 days in an airtight container.

You could decorate your cupcakes with holly leaves and berries made from marzipan. Find out how to make marzipan shapes on page 45.

Spiced apple muffins

These apple muffins will fill your kitchen with the Christmassy smells of cinnamon, cloves, orange and lemon.

Ingredients:

3 eating apples

$\frac{1}{2}$ cup (1 stick) butter

3 cloves

$1\frac{3}{4}$ cups self-rising flour

$1\frac{1}{2}$ teaspoons baking powder

$1\frac{1}{2}$ teaspoons ground cinnamon

$\frac{1}{4}$ cup cornflour

1 cup sugar

2 medium eggs

$\frac{3}{4}$ cup milk

For the topping:

1 small lemon

1 small orange

3 tablespoons decorator sugar

You will also need:

a 12-hole muffin tray

12 muffin cases (see page 46 to find out how to make your own)

❄ Makes 12 muffins.

Make sure the knife is facing away from you.

Stir every now and then.

1 Preheat the oven to 375°F. Put a paper case in each hole in the tray.

2 Use a peeler to peel the skin off an apple. Cut it into quarters. Put them on a board. Make two cuts in each one, in a V-shape, to cut out the core. Then, cut the quarters into small chunks.

3 Do the same with the other apples. Put them in a pan with the butter and cloves. Cook over low heat for 5 minutes. Turn off the heat.

4 In a large bowl, mix the flour, baking powder, cinnamon, cornflour and sugar. Beat the eggs and milk in a pitcher.

5 Use a wooden spoon to remove the cloves from the pan. Pour the apple mixture and the eggy mixture into the flour.

6 Stir until everything is just mixed. It should still look lumpy.

7

Spoon the mixture into the paper cases. Bake for 18-20 minutes until firm and golden.

8

Squeeze the juice from half the lemon and half the orange, and mix it with the sugar. Spoon over the muffins while they're still hot.

At step 4, you could add some of these if you like:

❋ a handful of raisins or dried cranberries

❋ a few chopped walnuts or pecans

These will keep for up to 2 days in an airtight container.

25

Christmas fruit cake

This Christmas cake is packed with fruit. First, make the cake, decorate it with marzipan and glaze, then cut it into little squares.

Ingredients:

10 tablespoons butter, softened

2/3 cup brown sugar

2 large eggs

1 orange

1 lemon

1 1/2 cups mixture of dried fruits, such as apricots, prunes and dates

1/2 cup dried cranberries

2 cups (9 oz.) mixture of currants, raisins and golden raisins

1 oz. chopped mixed peel (optional)

1 cup and 2 tablespoons all-purpose flour

1/2 teaspoon baking powder

2 teaspoons allspice

To decorate:

2 tablespoons smooth apricot jam

7 oz. package marzipan (optional)

2 tablespoons powdered sugar

4 tablespoons warm water

You will also need:

an 8 inch square cake pan

❄ Makes 25 squares.

1

Preheat the oven to 350°F. Line the pan with parchment. Cut another square of parchment the same size to use later.

2

Cut two strips of parchment 14 inches long and 5 inches wide. Use the strips to line the sides of the pan.

The mixture will look lumpy.

3

Beat the butter and sugar in a large bowl. Beat the eggs in a cup, then add them to the bowl a little at a time, beating well between each addition.

4

Grate the zest from the orange and lemon. Squeeze the juice from the orange. Add the zest and juice to the mixture.

5

Remove the date pits if there are any. Use scissors to snip the apricots, prunes and dates into small pieces. Add the fruit to the bowl.

6

Add the cranberries, currants, raisins, golden raisins, mixed peel, flour, baking powder and allspice. Mix it all together well.

You could decorate each square with a candied cherry. For more decorating ideas see pages 44-45.

These will keep for up to a month in an airtight container.

7

Spoon the mixture into the pan. Use the spoon to push it into the corners and smooth the top. Lay the square of parchment on top.

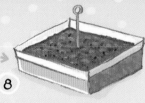

8

Bake for 50 minutes to an hour. Peel off the parchment. Push a skewer into the cake. If it comes out without cake stuck to it, it's ready.

9

Leave the cake in the pan until it's cool. Turn it onto a wire rack. Peel off the parchment. Spread jam over the cake.

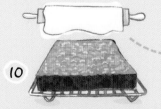

10

Roll out the marzipan until it is bigger than the cake. Fold it over the rolling pin and lift it onto the cake.

11

Use scissors to trim the edges off the marzipan. For the glaze, sift the powdered sugar into a bowl. Mix with the water. Spread over the cake.

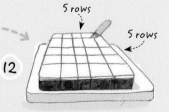

5 rows

5 rows

12

Leave the glaze to dry, then cut into 25 squares, using a sharp knife.

Kringle

This festive Danish bread is flavored with lemon and
filled with cinnamon butter.

Ingredients:

8 cardamom pods (optional)

2 lemons

2 ⅓ cups strong white
    bread flour

½ teaspoon salt

2 tablespoons sugar

2 teaspoons rapid rise yeast

¼ cup (½ stick) butter

½ cup milk

1 medium egg

For the cinnamon filling:

¼ cup (½ stick) butter, softened

¼ cup sugar

2 teaspoons ground cinnamon

1

If using, snip open the cardamom
pods. Crush the seeds with a
rolling pin. Grate the zest from
the lemons. Mix the seeds, zest,
flour, salt, sugar and yeast in a
large bowl.

2

Heat the butter and half
the milk in a pan until
the butter has melted.
Turn off the heat.

3

Beat the egg with the rest
of the milk in a pitcher.
Put a tablespoonful in a
cup for later.

4

Add the eggy mixture and
the buttery mixture to the
flour. Stir to make a dough.

5

To knead the dough, press
the heels of both hands
into it. Push it away from
you firmly. Fold it in half
and turn it around.

6

Continue pushing the dough away
from you, folding it and turning it
around for 10 minutes, until it feels
smooth and springy.

This Kringle is decorated with a drizzle of lemon glaze (see page 44) and some chopped candied cherries and pistachio nuts.

This will keep for up to 4 days in an airtight container.

7

It doesn't matter if the edges are wavy.

Roll the dough into a sausage shape about 16 inches long. Flatten it with rolling pin, so it is about 6 inches wide.

8

For the filling, beat the butter, sugar and cinnamon in a bowl. Spread over the dough, leaving a ³/₄ inch border around the edge.

9

Brush water along one long edge. Roll up the dough from the other long edge. Press firmly along the seam.

10

Put it onto a baking tray with the seam facing down. Shape into a large knot, tucking both ends under. Cover with a clean dish towel.

11

Leave in a warm place for 1-2 hours until it has risen to twice its original size. Preheat the oven to 400°F.

12

Take off the towel. Brush the dough with the eggy mixture you set aside. Bake for 25-30 minutes until golden. Put onto a wire rack to cool.

Christmas log

Christmas log is popular in France, where it is known as 'bûche de Noël'. Traditionally, at midwinter celebrations, a huge log was brought inside and burned on the fire. A Christmas log is often decorated to look like a real log.

Ingredients:

4 large eggs

$^2/_3$ cup sugar

$^1/_2$ cup ($2^1/_2$ oz.) ground almonds

2 tablespoons cocoa powder

$1^1/_4$ teaspoons baking powder

For the chocolate buttercream:

2 tablespoons butter, softened

1 cup powdered sugar

2 tablespoons milk

$^1/_2$ teaspoon vanilla

1 tablespoon cocoa powder

For the raspberry cream filling:

1 cup heavy whipping cream

6 oz. fresh raspberries

$1^1/_2$ tablespoons sugar

You will also need:

a 10 x 14 inch Swiss roll pan

1

Preheat the oven to 350° F. Grease and line the pan with baking parchment. Separate the eggs so the whites are in one bowl and the yolks are in another.

2

Beat the sugar with the yolks until they are pale and thick. Stir in the ground almonds, cocoa and baking powder.

3

Use an electric mixer to whisk the egg whites, until they are really thick. When you lift up the mixer, they should make stiff peaks, like this.

4

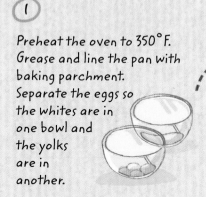

Gently fold the whites into the yolk mixture. Pour into the pan. Bake for 20-25 minutes until firm.

5

Leave in the pan for ten minutes. Cover it with a clean dish towel. Put it in the refrigerator for an hour.

6

For the buttercream, beat the butter and powdered sugar in a bowl until they are smooth. Mix the milk, vanilla and cocoa. Stir them into the buttercream.

7 For the filling, whip the cream (see page 42). Mash the raspberries with a fork. Stir them into the cream, with the sugar.

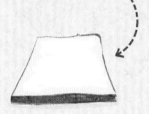

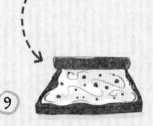

8 Take the cake out of the refrigerator. Run a knife around the edges. Sift some powdered sugar onto a surface. Turn the cake onto it.

This will keep for up to 3 days in the refrigerator, in an airtight container.

9 Peel the parchment off the top of the cake. Spread the filling over the cake. Carefully roll it up from one of the short ends. Lift it onto a plate.

10 Spread the chocolate buttercream all over the cake.

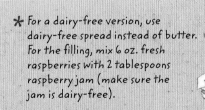

* For a dairy-free version, use dairy-free spread instead of butter. For the filling, mix 6 oz. fresh raspberries with 2 tablespoons raspberry jam (make sure the jam is dairy-free).

* To make it gluten-free and wheat-free, use gluten-free and wheat-free baking powder.

You could sift over powdered sugar and decorate your Christmas log with fresh mint leaves and raspberries.

Maple cupcakes

These cupcakes are flavored with maple syrup and topped with a swirl of buttercream frosting. They are delicious made with or without pecans.

Ingredients:

1/2 cup (2 oz.) pecans (optional)

1/2 cup (1 stick) butter, softened

1/4 cup soft light brown sugar

7/8 cup self-rising flour

2 medium eggs

6 tablespoons maple syrup

For the buttercream frosting:

2 tablespoons butter, softened

1 cup powdered sugar

2 tablespoons milk

1/2 teaspoon vanilla

You will also need:

a 12-hole muffin tray

12 paper cupcake cases

❄ Makes 12 cupcakes.

If you are adding pecans, put them in a plastic food bag and seal the end. Crush them into small pieces with a rolling pin.

1 Preheat the oven to 375°F. Beat the butter and sugar in a large bowl until they are light and fluffy. Sift in the flour.

2 Beat the eggs in a cup. Add them to the bowl, with the pecans and maple syrup. Stir until everything is well mixed.

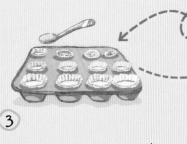

3 Put a paper case in each hole in the tray. Use a small spoon to divide the mixture between the paper cases. Bake for 12-15 minutes until risen and firm.

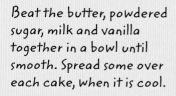

4 Leave in the tray for a few minutes. Lift each one onto a wire rack to cool. Meanwhile, make the buttercream.

5 Beat the butter, powdered sugar, milk and vanilla together in a bowl until smooth. Spread some over each cake, when it is cool.

These will keep for up to 5 days in an airtight container.

You could decorate your cupcakes with nuts, candies or sprinkles. Make different colors of icing, by adding one or two drops of food dye to the buttercream.

33

Lebkuchen

These German cookies have a soft, chewy texture and a spicy flavor. Traditionally, they are round and covered with a very thin glaze, but you can often find them in other shapes, such as hearts.

Ingredients:

¹/₂ cup all-purpose flour

¹/₂ teaspoon baking powder

¹/₂ teaspoon cinnamon

1 teaspoon allspice

¹/₃ cup soft light brown sugar

¹/₃ cup ground almonds

2 medium eggs

3 soft dates

3 tablespoons (2 oz.) marzipan

3 tablespoons smooth apricot jam

2 oz. chopped mixed peel

²/₃ cup (4 oz.) whole blanched almonds

For the glaze:

¹/₄ cup powdered sugar

2 teaspoons water

❄ Makes around 12 cookies.

① Put the flour, baking powder, cinnamon and allspice in a large bowl. Stir in the sugar and ground almonds.

② Break the eggs into a cup or a small bowl and beat them with a fork. Cut the dates in half. Take out the pits if there are any.

③ Put the dates in another large bowl and mash them with a fork. Mix 1 tablespoon of egg into the dates.

④ Crumble the marzipan into the date mixture. Add the jam and mash everything together.

⑤ Stir in the rest of the eggs, a little at a time. Add the mixed peel and the floury mixture. Mix everything together well.

These will keep for up to 5 days in an airtight container.

(6) Cover the bowl with plastic foodwrap and put it in the refrigerator for 30 minutes. Preheat the oven to 325°F.

Space well apart.

(7) Line two trays with parchment. Use a small spoon to drop round blobs of the mixture onto the trays. Arrange 3 almonds on top of each blob.

(8) Bake for 15 minutes until lightly browned. Leave on the trays for 5 minutes, then put on a wire rack to cool.

(9) For the glaze, sift the powdered sugar into a bowl. Stir in the water. Brush over the cookies.

The glaze on these cookies is so thin, you can hardly see it.

Chocolate Christmas cake

This rich chocolate orange cake is packed with nuts. If you don't like dried fruits, this makes a delicious alternative to traditional Christmas fruit cake.

Ingredients:

1 large orange

8 oz. bar semi-sweet or milk chocolate

12 oz. unsalted almonds, hazelnuts and walnuts, preferably pre-chopped

7/8 cup sugar

2 tablespoons butter

5 large eggs

You will also need:

an 8 inch spring form pan

If you can't get pre-chopped nuts, put whole nuts in a plastic food bag and seal the end. Crush them into small pieces with a rolling pin.

1 Preheat the oven to 350°F. Grease and line the pan with baking parchment. Grate the zest from the orange and squeeze out the juice.

2 Cut the chocolate into small pieces. Put the chocolate, zest, nuts and sugar into a large bowl.

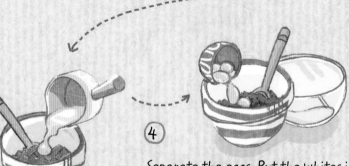

3 Heat the butter in a pan until it melts. Turn off the heat and add the orange juice. Add the buttery mixture to the ingredients in the bowl. Stir everything together.

4 Separate the eggs. Put the whites into a large, clean bowl. Add the yolks to the chocolate mixture and stir them in.

This will keep for up to a week, covered with foil or foodwrap.

⑤ Whisk the egg whites with an electric mixer until they are really thick. They should make stiff peaks, like this.

⑥ Add two large spoonfuls of egg white to the chocolate mixture. Use a metal spoon to fold them in gently. Add the rest of the whites and fold them in.

Peel off the parchment.

You could sift powdered sugar over your cake in a doily pattern. See page 44 to find out how.

⑦ Spoon the mixture into the pan. Bake the cake for one hour.

⑧ Push a skewer into the middle of the cake. When it comes out without cake mixture stuck to it, it is ready. Leave it in the pan for 10 minutes, then turn it onto a wire rack.

Gingerbread houses

Making houses out of gingerbread is a tradition that began in Germany, inspired by the gingerbread house in the fairy tale 'Hansel and Gretel'. You can use any candy, sprinkles, or other decorations on your gingerbread houses.

Ingredients:

1½ cups all-purpose flour

1½ teaspoons ground ginger

½ teaspoon ground cinnamon

1 teaspoon baking soda

½ cup (1 stick) butter, chilled

¾ cup light brown sugar

1 medium egg

2 tablespoons corn syrup

writing icing, candy and sprinkles for decorating

❄ Makes around 10 houses.

① Preheat the oven to 350°F. Line two baking trays with parchment or use non-stick cooking spray. Mix the flour, ginger, cinnamon and baking soda in a large bowl.

② Cut the butter into chunks. Rub it into the flour until the mixture looks like breadcrumbs. Stir in the sugar.

③ Break the egg into a small bowl and mix in the syrup. Add it to the flour. Stir everything together, then squeeze it into a smooth dough.

Dust a rolling pin and surface with flour.

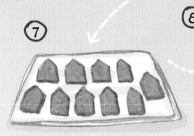

④ Roll out the dough, until it is as thick as your little finger.

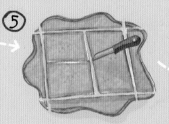

⑤ Cut off the wobbly edges with a sharp knife, to make a square. Then, cut the square into four pieces, like this.

⑥ Cut each piece in half, to make a rectangle. Then, cut a triangle from the top corners of each rectangle, to make house shapes.

⑦ Squeeze the scraps into a ball, roll it out and cut more houses. Put them onto the trays. Bake for 12-15 minutes until dark golden.

⑧ Leave the houses on the trays for a few minutes, then put on a wire rack to cool. Decorate with writing icing and press on candy and sprinkles.

These will keep for up to 5 days in an airtight container.

You could cover a whole cookie with glaze (see page 44 for the glaze recipe). Leave the glaze to dry, then draw on top with writing icing.

Stollen

This fruit bread has a marzipan filling, which represents the baby Jesus wrapped in blankets. It has been eaten at Christmas in Germany for over 500 years.

Ingredients:

1 lemon

1/4 cup (2 oz.) candied cherries

1/3 cup (2 oz.) almonds

3 cups strong white bread flour

1 teaspoon salt

1 teaspoon allspice

3 tablespoons sugar

2 teaspoons rapid rise yeast

2/3 cup (4 oz.) mixture of currants, raisins and golden raisins

1 tablespoon (1 oz.) chopped mixed peel

4 tablespoons (1/2 stick) butter

3/4 cup and 2 tablespoons milk

For the marzipan filling:

1 medium egg

5 tablespoons sugar

1/3 cup (2 oz.) ground almonds

①

Grate the zest from the lemon. Cut the cherries and almonds into small pieces. Put them into a large bowl with the zest.

②

Put the flour, salt, allspice, sugar, yeast, dried fruit and peel into the large bowl. Mix them together.

③

Put the butter and half the milk in a pan. Heat gently until the butter has just melted. Take off the heat, then add the rest of the milk.

④

Pour the milky mixture into the bowl. Stir to make a dough.

⑤

To knead the dough, follow steps 4 and 5 on page 28. Then, press the dough into an oblong shape, about 8 x 10 inches.

⑥

For the filling, break the egg into a bowl. Stir in the sugar and ground almonds. Spread it down the middle of the dough.

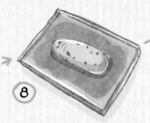

7

Fold in the two shorter edges over the filling. Then fold over one long edge, then the other.

8

Lift onto a greased baking tray with the join facing down.

9

Cover with a clean dish towel. Leave in a warm place for 1-2 hours until it has risen to twice its original size.

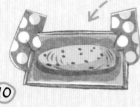

10

Preheat the oven to 350°F. Remove the dish towel. Cover with baking parchment and bake for 35-40 minutes until lightly browned.

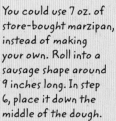

11

Leave on a wire rack for a few minutes to cool. You could sift powdered sugar over the top.

You could use 7 oz. of store-bought marzipan, instead of making your own. Roll into a sausage shape around 9 inches long. In step 6, place it down the middle of the dough.

This will keep for up to 5 days in an airtight container.

Toppings and fillings

You could use this whipped cream topping to make the raspberry cream filling for the Christmas log. Or try the orange cream or chocolate cream instead. The buttercream is for decorating the cakes and cookies, and the mincemeat is to fill mince pies.

Whipped cream topping

1. Pour 1 cup heavy cream into a bowl and add ¹/₄ cup sugar. Hold the bowl in one hand and use an electric mixer to whip the cream.

2. Continue until the cream starts to form stiff peaks when you lift the mixer, but stop before it becomes too solid.

Orange cream

Grate the zest from an orange. Put it in a bowl with 8 oz. (1 cup) cream cheese. Sift over ¹/₄ cup powdered sugar. Mix together.

Chocolate cream

Put 1 cup whipped cream into a bowl and stir in 3 tablespoons chocolate syrup. Refrigerate for 30 minutes before adding to your cakes.

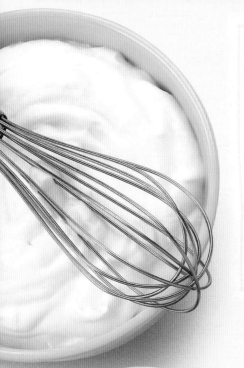

Buttercream frosting

2 tablespoons soft butter
(or dairy-free spread)

1 cup powdered sugar

2 tablespoons milk (or soy
or lactose-free milk)

1/2 teaspoon vanilla

① Beat the butter with a wooden spoon until it is soft and creamy. Sift over about a third of the sugar. Stir it in.

② Sift over the rest of the sugar. Add the milk and vanilla. Beat everything until it is pale and fluffy.

For colored buttercream, pour 1-2 drops of food dye onto a teaspoon. Stir them in after you have beaten the buttercream.

For chocolate buttercream, mix 1 tablespoon of cocoa with the milk. Add it to the mixture at step 2.

Mincemeat

If you are allergic to nuts, just leave them out.

1 orange

1 lemon

1/2 cup (3 oz.) seedless grapes

2 1/2 tablespoons hazelnuts

1 apple

ground cinnamon,
    nutmeg and ginger

1 cup (5 oz.) raisins

① Grate the zest from the orange and lemon. Chop the grapes and hazelnuts into small pieces.

② Don't bother peeling the apple. Use the large holes of the grater to grate it. Stop when you get to the core.

③ Put the zest, grapes, nuts and apple in a bowl. Stir in the raisins and a pinch each of cinnamon, nutmeg and ginger.

Decorating ideas

There are lots of different ways you can decorate your cakes and cookies. Here are some ideas for different types of glaze, sugar patterns and marzipan decorations.

Glaze

1 ⅓ cups powdered sugar

1½ tablespoons warm water

(Or follow the quantities in the recipe you are using.)

① Sift the powdered sugar into a bowl. Stir in the warm water to make a smooth paste.

② Use a teaspoon to scoop up some glaze and spread it onto a cake or cookie. For a smooth surface, dip a blunt knife into some warm water and slide it over the glaze.

Colored glaze

For colored glaze, measure 1 or 2 drops of food dye onto a teaspoon, then stir it into the glaze. Add more for a darker color.

Lemon glaze

For lemon glaze, replace the water with 1½ tablespoons of lemon juice. Or use orange or tangerine juice instead.

Doily designs

Lay a doily over a cake. Sift powdered sugar or cocoa over it. Carefully lift off the doily.

Stencil patterns

① Take a piece of paper that's bigger than your cake. Fold it in half. Draw half a shape against the fold. Cut it out.

② Unfold the paper and lay it over your cake. Sift a little powdered sugar or cocoa over it. Carefully lift off the stencil.

You could also use the cut-out shape from the middle of your stencil, like this.

Homemade sugar sprinkles

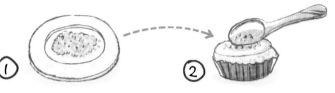

① Put 1 tablespoon of granulated sugar onto a plate. Add 1 or 2 drops of food dye and mix it in. Spread it onto a plate to dry.

② Use the back of a spoon to break up the sugar. Then, scoop it up and sprinkle it onto an iced cake.

You could use a stencil with some sugar sprinkles, too.

Marzipan shapes

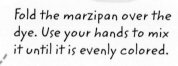

① Put some 'white' marzipan into a bowl. Make a hollow in it and drop in 1 or 2 drops of food dye.

② Fold the marzipan over the dye. Use your hands to mix it until it is evenly colored.

③ Put the marzipan onto a clean surface. Roll it out with a rolling pin. Use cookie cutters to cut out the shapes you want.

For candy canes, roll out two sticks of red and white marzipan. Twist them together, roll again, then shape into a cane.

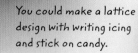

You could make a lattice design with writing icing and stick on candy.

Wrapping ideas

Cookies and cakes can make perfect Christmas presents. You could put them in a wrapped food box or tin, or try out the pretty packaging ideas below.

Some of the recipes in this book keep better than others. Check the recipe to find out how long you can keep each thing, and the best way to store it.

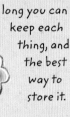

Jar lid cover

① Find a plate or saucer around 2 inches wider than your jar lid. Put the plate on some decorated paper or material and draw around it. Then, cut it out.

② Put it over the jar lid. Press the edges down over the lid and secure it with a rubber band. Then tie some pretty ribbon or string around it.

Muffin cases

① For each muffin, cut a square of baking parchment around 5 inches across. Lay it over a hole in a muffin tray. Push it in, squashing until it fits.

② Spoon in the muffin mix and bake. When your muffins have cooled, you could tie some ribbon or string around them.

Index

Additional design and cover by Nancy Leschnikoff

Photography by Howard Allman

Edited by Abigail Wheatley and Jane Chisholm   Art Director: Mary Cartwright

Food preparation by Dagmar Vesely, Abigail Wheatley and Nelupa Hussain   Digital imaging: Nick Wakeford

Every effort has been made to trace the copyright holders of material in this book. If any rights have been omitted, the publishers offer to rectify this in any subsequent editions following notification.